Contents

Introduction

The Border Collie originated from the British Isles, and spent much of its developing history in the border country of Britain and Scotland, hence the first part of its official name. The second part, "Collie" has less certain origins. It may come from the word "coalie", meaning black, a Gaelic work meaning "useful", or from the name of a particular Scottish sheep breed. No matter the specific origins of its name, all these terms represent important aspects of this breed.

The Border Collie was selectively bred for its skill in herding sheep, which includes its ability to use its eye to intimidate sheep. The Border Collie is still used for herding sheep in Britain and the U.S. It is also known for its high performance in agility trials.

Chapter one

The Complete Breed Compatibility Guide for Border Collies

The Puppy Mag is an Amazon associate and earns a small commission for qualifying purchases. We also work with other affiliate programs so please assume all links are affiliate links. The following information is for educational purposes only.

If you've got a Border collie and are considering getting another dog, it's very important to pick a compatible breed. All breeds have different personalities and behavioral tendencies, so choosing the correct one may not be so simple.

Whether you're getting a new dog, or you're just curious to know which breeds get along well with Border Collies, this article has everything you need to know. Let's get into it!

Key Points about a Border Collies' Character

Before thinking about other breeds, it's important to understand the basic characteristics of Border Collies themselves.

When it comes to humans, opposites may attract, but in the dog world, this usually doesn't end too well. So we must first know the typical facts about Border Collies.

Most of the points outlined below will be accurate for the majority of Border Collies, but yours may well be different. That's okay, as long as you consider that when choosing another breed.

1. Collies Have A LOT of Energy and Require A LOT of Exercise

Border collies are hard-working dogs that have a tonne of energy. They were bred to work on farms and herd sheep, and they're at the top of their game. Collies need 1-2 hours of exercise per day and will even continue to play throughout the day.

Some breeds are the complete opposite of this, English Bulldogs, for example, would rather lay down on the couch than go for a walk. A breed like this likely isn't going to be much fun for your collie and it may eventually get in the way of her vigorous exercise routine.

An athletic breed ideally needs to have an athletic buddy.

2. Rough Play with Nipping

Border Collies and other herding-breeds have developed a tendency to nip. It's an effective tactic to keep sheep going in the direction they want them to, but it carries over to everyday life.

Hopefully, this behavior has already been trained against before you get another dog, but it helps that the other dog can "keep their own" so to speak.

Some dogs hate engaging in rough play and a Collie may be too much for many breeds to handle. Not only would this be unfair for the new dog, but it won't bode well for a good relationship. Your second dog needs to be strong and like rough play.

3. Intelligent With Working Desires

Border Collies are the world's most intelligent dogs. They love to be trained, follow commands, have a desire to work and be useful, and are extremely obedient.

If you were to get a dog that's notoriously disobedient and troublesome the chances are that your Collie's current level of greatness, will drop a little.

While it's not mandatory to get a dog that's as smart as a Border collie, it will without a doubt lead to a stronger bond between the two dogs if you do. Not to mention, your life will be easier.

4. Prey Drive / Herding Tendencies

One of the most notable behavioral traits of Border Collies is their ability and desire to herd. When there are no sheep around, it's not uncommon for collies to even try herding their human-family.

Herding is actually considered a modified version of the prey drive and smaller animals including tiny dog breeds could be at risk when left alone with a Border Collie (especially in the early stages).

Of course, there are many examples of Border Collies that wouldn't hurt a fly, but when you get a new dog in the household that hasn't yet established their place in the pack, it cannot be overlooked. More on this later.

10 Breeds that get along well with a Border collie

Below we're going to cover 10 breeds that Border Collies get along well with. These breeds share the same personality and behavioral traits as the Border collie.

Each breed on the list will come with a short explanation of why they would work well with a Border collie.

1. German Shepherd

German shepherds are extremely similar to Border Collies and are often considered an ideal companion breed.

German shepherds are not only extremely intelligent, they love to learn, follow commands and have a great work ethic. These two dogs will compliment each other in their learning and obedience.

GSD's also require a lot of exercise, most have high energy, and they will certainly hold their own during rough-play. If you have an active household, a German shepherd will be a great second dog for your Border Collie.

2. Australian Shepherd

Aussies are becoming forever more popular and are making their way into more households every year. Despite being named "Australian" Shepherds, they have no association with Australia and were bred in California as herding dogs to work on ranches.

Aussies are very intelligent, love to follow commands, work, herd (just like collies) and they're a great all-round family dog with a lot of affection to give.

An Australian Shepherd will match up perfectly in size and character with your Border collie. Just be extra cautious if you have young children, two herding dogs may become overwhelming for kids. So this is certainly something to think about.

3. Standard Poodle

Poodles come in all shapes and sizes, but it's the standard Poodle that matches up particularly well with Border Collies.

Standard Poodles are very similar in size to a Border Collie and will hold their own when engaging in a little rough play.

Poodles are actually second on the list of the most intelligent dog breeds, so it goes without saying their trainability, obedience and willingness to follow commands is perfectly inline with a Collie.

They also have high energy and require just as much exercise as a Border Collie. Poodles often make great family dogs and are considered to be an all-round breed. Definitely a great match up for most Collies out there.

4. Golden Retriever

The Golden Retriever is arguably the world's most-loved breed and they are considered to be one of the best "all-round" breeds.

They're incredibly friendly, loving, kind as well as being energetic, highly intelligent, and obedient.

A Golden Retriever will make a great partner with any Border collie and they'll be a great matchup.

If at any time you've considered getting a Golden Retriever, then think no further, this breed will be the ideal addition to your family.

5. Dalmatian

Dalmatians may be one of the very few breeds that require more exercise than a Border collie. This high-energy breed used to run alongside horse and carriage across the country.

By nature, Dalmatians make great companions for both humans and other canines, so there likely won't be an issue in the two dogs getting along well.

Although intelligent, Dalmatians have a mischievous and stubborn streak in them, so this breed would require more time and attention to ensure good-behavior.

As long as you have the time to train this breed, a Dalmatian will be a great addition to the family.

6. Labrador

Labradors are extremely similar to Golden Retrievers, in that they are very kind, affectionate, good-natured, intelligent and highly active.

Getting a Labrador is another safe bet if you're unsure on which breed will work well for both your Collie and your family.

Labradors although intelligent, do have it in them to be unruly if not properly trained.

A Lab will certainly make the best playmate for your Collie and will hold their own in rough play.

7. English Pointer

English pointers are significantly decreasing in popularity, but not because of anything bad. In fact, English Pointers are considered to be an all-round breed, being affectionate, kind, intelligent, loyal, and easy to train.

A Pointer will be your Border Collies perfect exercise partner as they are similar in size and have matching amounts of energy and desire to play.

If you're not worried about the declining numbers of the English Pointer population, this is a good breed to consider.

8. Belgian Tervuren (Belgian Shepherd)

Belgian Shepherds are very similar to both Border Collies and German Shepherds. They are fairly larger than a Border collie so you'll need to be happy with getting a big dog.

Belgian Shepherds are strong, loyal, and protective dogs, and are very similar to German Shepherds. Their courage and guard dog capabilities are also met with equal amounts of love and affection.

They are highly energetic and will require just as much exercise as a Collie.

If you're looking for a large second dog that's easily trained, the Belgian Shepherd could be for you.

9. Boxer

The Boxer is a highly-energetic breed that loves to play and is very capable of holding their own. They need just as much, if not more exercise than a Border Collie, so your situation should allow for that.

The Boxer stands tall and will grow to be bigger than your Border Collie. Boxers have short coats that hardly shed at all, especially compared to a Border Collie!

Boxers are intelligent but they are known to have a mischievous streak in them and training is very important.

An untrained Boxer can be unruly and may even encourage your Border Collie to take part in bad-behavior too. So training is paramount.

10. Siberian Husky

The Siberian husky usually raises a lot of eyebrows, and rightfully so, huskies are by far the least similar to Border Collies on this list, but there's a reason why they are added.

Huskies and Border Collies seem to just get along, time and time again. They are each other's favorite dog at the play parks, and I've seen countless Husky / Collie households.

Their energy levels, desire to play, and work are all matched. Not to mention they are of similar physical size too.

Huskies are, however, hard to train and although very intelligent, will often choose to be stubborn and mischievous. Training a husky is tough, but rewarding.

This pair is only recommended if you're truly ready for a lot of work, but if you are, it will be one of the best match-ups.

This is original content produced and published by The Puppy Mag | www.thepuppymag.com | If this content appears on any other website or platform then it is not the original and action will be taken.

Summary of Characteristics That Suit Border Collies

This list only contains 10 other breeds, but there are far more out there. So this list below will summarize the characteristics found in other breeds that will naturally work well for your Border Collie.

The following traits found in compatible breeds:

Similar in size

Intelligent and trainable

Naturally sociable

Enjoys rough play

Naturally obedient

Not overly territorial

Affectionate

Requires a lot of exercise

Enjoying working and having a job to fulfill

Breeds that have most of the above qualities, will likely get on well with a Border Collie, and your family.

But it's important to remember that all dogs are different, and sometimes individual behavior may not fall in-line with breed stereotypes.

Are Border Collies Better in Pairs

What about two Border Collies? So far this article has been about different breeds, but if you're interested in two Collies, read on.

Like with most breeds, they are often better off in pairs. They are able to keep each other company, and dogs are pack animals after all.

It's likely that each Collie will be extremely similar, which instantly bodes well for a strong relationship that will make each dog happy.

According to science, a dog is happier when they have another canine companion around them.

It's yet to be confirmed whether dogs recognize their own breed or not. So whether your Collie actually knows their new friend is another Collie will never be known. But the chances of them getting along are very high.

Do Border Collies Get Along With Small Dogs

As mentioned earlier, the prey drive of a Border Collie needs to be considered before choosing a small or tiny breed.

Disclaimer: we know that there are countless examples of Border Collies and small dogs getting along harmoniously. And it's entirely possible for your Border Collie too.

However, it can't be overlooked that the herding trait (which is a modified form of the prey drive) is extremely strong in Border Collies. So much so, that they will try to herd humans when there's nothing left to herd. That's pretty significant.

Naturally, dogs with high prey drives (herding or not) have the ability to chase and in some instances even kill small animals like rabbits, squirrels and small dogs are no exception.

Border Collies do not have a reputation for killing small dogs, but they do have a very strong prey drive in them and are physically capable of doing so.

If you really want a small breed for your second dog you'll need to take extra precaution for a long time before you can be confident that the two dogs have an established relationship.

So yes, Border Collies can get along with small breeds, so long as extra precaution is taken, and their general behavior traits match-up as explained above.

The Best Way to Know Which Breed Your Border Collie Will Like

One of the best ways to know what breed your Border Collie will like is to visit doggy play centers, and your local park (more than you already are).

Going to the park or dedicated doggy play sessions will give you a chance to observe your Collie interact with other breeds.

Do this for one or two months and you will see a clear pattern between the kinds of breeds your Collie gravitates towards.

You may see a pattern that your Collie does in fact play very well and gently with smaller breeds, or you may witness your Collie consistently avoiding smaller breeds. You may see that your Collie frequently chooses to play Labradors above all other breeds.

This is truly the best way to find compatible breeds for your Collie.

If you are thinking about breeding Border Collies, you probably know that you are about the breed the smartest dog breed ever. The Border collie is a graceful, intelligent and athletic dog. It is known for his incredible herding instinct as well as for its mind-boggling agility.

Border Collies also tend to be extremely loyal and whether you are looking for a working dog breed or an agility breed, the Border collie must be at the top of your list. They excel at everything they do in the ring, in trials, and on the field.

Given their obedience and responsiveness to training, Border Collies also make for great police dogs as many countries are starting to test them. They are also incredible companions for blind people.

In a nutshell, wondering how to breed Border Collies is very normal; and you will not regret it!

This article will help you with the ins and outs of becoming a Border collie breeder.

History of the Border collie

The roots of the word "collie" are hotly disputed. The term "Border Collie" itself is believed to have been used for the first time around 1915 in the United Kingdom. Among the myriad of sources that the term is attributed to, one of the most plausible explanation seems to be that it is derived from the German language. The term kuli, which has been argued to be the basis for the term collie, translates to a worker in English. When we consider that the Border collie is a working dog breed, then this seems to make perfect sense.

Another plausible origin of the term is the fact that the Border Collie is believed to have its origins in a place called Northumberland in

England. As some of you may know, this is a place that is on the border between England and Scotland. Therefore, this explanation is also very plausible. It is virtually impossible to be certain about such things because of all the time that has passed. However, the mountains between near the border of England and Scotland, as well as the extraordinary herding instinct of the breed lead everybody to believe that Northumberland is the birthplace of the Border Collie.

The First Border Collie Studs

The breed can be traced back to one primary source, The Old Hemp, who is known as the Father of the Border Collie breed. The Old Hemp is attributed with staggering feats and all pure Border Collies alive today can trace an ancestral line back to the wonderful Old Hemp.

Old hemp Border collie history

Wiston Cap is another associated breed which is believed to have influenced the Border collie, and the Collie breed, with his bloodline appearing in most bloodlines of the modern-day Collie.

The Border collie has an intrinsic sense of herding; therefore, it was the ideal herding dog for livestock. Historically, the Border collie has gained prominence because it requires minimal human guidance and is known for its high performance. Border Collies have the ability to toil long hours which makes it one of the most preferred working dogs in the world.

Best Practices When Breeding Border Collies

Every dog breeder must pay due attention to best practices and it is no different with breeders of the "Border Collie". There are broad rules you must follow, without which you will be unable to get the best out of your Border collie and this will end up having a detrimental effect on your relationship with your dog.

Coats, Colors & Patterns

The Border collie breed is allowed to have very different coat types, coat colors, and patterns. It can be difficult to understand as we're often just aware of the black and white border collies, but there are plenty more.

Firstly, the allowed coat types are:

Rough Coat — moderate and extreme rough coats are found within the breed, with a shorter length on the belly

Smooth Coat — the short-haired Border Collies allowing to showcase a beautiful structure

Curly Coat — very rare, but nonetheless existing, are the curly-coated Border Collies

Bearded — extremely rare, too, is the bearded variety of purebred Border collie

Several coat colors and patterns are allowed when breeding Border Collies:

Black & White — the most common, and arguably 'classic', color combination in the entire breed

Tri-Colored — other most occurring pattern, tricolor collies may come in every other color but usually black, white and tan

Red & White — also called chocolate and white, this pattern is currently rising in popularity

Sable & White — rarer nowadays, the tan coat with black tips used to be common in the 19th century

Blue & White — a genetically complex color, blue is often a recessive dilute blue-grey

Lilac — rare color that is brown and blue at the same time, and it is a double dilute

Merle — more of a pattern than color as you can have red merle, blue merle, slate merle, sable merle, etc.

In all honesty, there are even more color combinations, as well as coat types, within the Border Collie breed and it's would be hard to list them all. The BC Museum is a good place to read more about the various coats in the breed.

Border collie Coats

Info graphic: the most common coat colors and patterns in Border Collies

Such an enormous number of coat variations is because the Border collie has always been, first and foremost, a working breed. Therefore, appearance and looks generally mattered very little, if at all. With time, showing and agility lines have gained in popularity to the point of being the "mainstream Border Collie" today, with all combinations now part of the breed.

Size, Weight & Average Litter Size

Certainly not the biggest dogs in the world, Border Collies fall somewhere in the medium-sized category. The average height of a Border collie is about 20 inches; the average weight is about 30-45 pounds.

Male Border Collies do tend to be bigger in size than their female counterparts, but not by much. Equally, the female Border Collies are also slightly lighter than their male counterparts. The difference in both height and weight between the male and female Border Collies is not significant enough for them to be grouped into different categories.

C-Section

Usually, vets will leave the choice of whether or not to perform a C-Section up to you unless it is an emergency and C-Section has to be performed at all costs. Always ensure that you do have a bit of extra money when your Border Collie is pregnant just in case you end up having to go for an emergency C-Section.

Rigorous Training Needed

The first thing that breeders need to bear in mind when it comes to Border Collies is that they are not the typical cuddly dogs that you can just keep at home all day. Furthermore, the odd short walk thrown in three times a day won't cut it either, unless trained from a very young age.

Border Collies are extremely active and require a tremendous amount of activity for their own natural well-being. They need to be trained regularly and it would be prudent to start their training as early as possible. Indeed, professionals have shown that dogs respond better to commands, and training in general when it is done at an early age. Intuitively it does make sense even human beings are advised to learn languages and skills at a young age as it tends to be easier to pick up things at that time in general.

Low Maintenance

Another comforting factor from the perspective of someone who is looking to breed a Border Collie is that it is not even close to being a high maintenance dog. You do not have to vigorously brush it day in and day out. However, weekly brushing is ideal especially during the shedding season if you have a rough-coated Border Collie.

Frequent baths are not necessary unless you work a lot outdoors with your dog. For everybody else, bathing your Border collie once every few months should be more than adequate in most cases. In between baths, the use of dog wipes can come in very handy!

Ear cleaning and tooth brushing of your Border Collie should be given considerable importance. This is where bacteria are most likely to form and cause your dog to fall sick, one way or another.

Diet

Given the very active nature of Border Collies that we mentioned earlier. Therefore, it is imperative that they are given a diet that is high in protein and healthy fats (omega-3 and omega-6 fatty acids) in order to maintain their muscle mass. Of course, an unbalanced diet high in protein could cause more harm than good, therefore a balanced diet is important.

The exact needs will differ from dog to dog depending on each individual's activity level and metabolism.

Because Border Collie are naturally up for all activities, as demanding as they can be, it is important to provide from an early age a good amount of supplementation to prevent dog arthritis at a later stage in life. This is the best way to strengthen your Border collie's joints and bones.

Health Concerns When Breeding Border Collies

The average life expectancy of a Border collie is about 12 to 15 years. This life expectancy could be cut short by multiple conditions, therefore, please ensure that you get the necessary health checks and clearances before breeding your border collie.

First and foremost, you should never ever breed two merle Border Collies together. Breeding merle-to-merle will inevitably cause deafness as well as vision problems in future generations, because of genetic conflict. Breeding merle-to-merle Border Collies is only done by irresponsible and ignorant puppy farmers. Generally, to get merle in a Border collie litter, a breeder has to breed for that color (which is fine, as long as it is not by breeding two merles together.)

Example of a Blue Merle Border collie

The Collie Eye Anomaly is one of the worst possible conditions that affects Border Collies. Although the risk rate is not overly high, there is virtually no way to detect this condition. If your dog shows signs of blindness, take it to the vet as soon as possible.

The breed is also vulnerable to Idiopathic Epilepsy, a rather common inherited medical condition in Border Collies. The typical symptoms generally appear between 1 year and 4 years of age; usually through visible twitches, seizures, or convulsions. Such fits can be worrying and you need to address the situation with your vet from the first time you notice them. Although the dog's welfare is rarely the core of the issue, such seizures and convulsions may put the dog in a harmful situation and is often terrorizing the dog, who now lives in fear and anxiety.

Hip dysplasia is somewhat prevalent among Border Collies, especially when breeders don't score their breeding stock. Hip and elbow dysplasias are almost impossible to eradicate, and can often only be soothed using medication.

Future of the Border collie Breed

As mentioned earlier, historically, the Border Collies were used primarily as a working breed. Their innate sense of herding made them the most popular sheepdog. In fact, so intrinsic is a Border collie's herding mentality that it has tendencies to herd cars, children, and anything that is moving as a group. In a nutshell, it was seen as the perfect farmer's dog. However, this is rapidly changing.

Although the instinct of a Border collie paired with its loyalty will always make it a great working breed, more and more dog breeders have preferred to use agility training methods to train their Border Collies. As you have seen earlier, Border Collies are incredibly smart, fast, and reactive. This makes them ideal for agility training. In addition to that, Border Collies are highly intelligent which means they can find their way around obstacles which is so essential when it comes to agility breeds.

Such intelligence is often thought to have originated after generations of selective breeding when farmers wanted very smart dogs to work with at a long distance.

Simply put, Border Collies have gone from being seen as a herding breed to being seen as an agility breed. You will not see a list of the best agility breeds without finding a mention of the Border Collie somewhere at the top (generally first.) This is not to say that they are no longer used for herding, but there has been a shift in their overall usage to agility training and in their image seen as an agility breed.

Border collie

Wish to adopt a dog that can outsmart you? Border Collie is where you stop. Border collie breed tops the list of world's smartest dogs and is known for his "stare".

Highly trainable and intelligent, they have proved themselves in every walks of canine sports from agility to fly ball and tracking. Though they are the smartest dogs, it is not easy to train them. You cannot laze around with this breed. They need constant dynamic training to polish their smartness.

Originally bred to herd sheep in the farms of Scotland, they are dogs with utmost stamina and an unstoppable workhorse. They are very active and are best suited for country life. They will only sit calmly when they have done enough for the day and will demand a lot of attention and cuddles thereafter.

If you do not have the stamina to out-run, and the brains to out-with him, you better reconsider your ideas of adopting a Collie.

The breed originally flourished on the England-Scotland border, where they herded sheep. That's how the "Border Collie" moniker was born; "collie" is a Scottish word for the sheepdog.

Size – Medium

This is a medium-sized dog that does not grow more than 19-22 inches for males and 18-21 inches for females in height. Border collie weight can vary from 30 to 45 pounds depending on gender. Female Border collie dog weight is 26 to 42 pounds and for males, it can be anything between 31 to 45 pounds.

A medium-sized dog with not more than 45 pounds in weight and 22 inches at the shoulder, Border collie possesses double the amount of stamina and energy. They were bred as sheepdogs in the rough terrains of England-Scotland border. Their regular work was running more than 50 miles a day. It makes then an ideal dog for country living.

It is a highly trainable dog who can learn a command in 5 repetitions and have proved to respond 95% of the time. They make an obedient and wonderful companion dog. They are great family dogs but it might get tiring (don't let your dog read this) to keep up with the amount of mental and physical exercise that they need. If you are looking for a cuddly-cute couch potato then Border collie may not be the right choice.

They are known for "the eye", a practice of staring intensely into the eyes of the sheep to control them. So, the next time you see your Collie gaping at you, you do not really need to worry. They are just trying to hypnotize you.

They have a habit of nipping at the herd. This overwhelming urge can come out when they see cats, children, or other small or moving things, which makes them an absolute no-no for small children. Border collie dog is very reserved and shy and may not be able to make friends. However, they can gel in with cats and other dogs pretty well if brought up together.

It is not very easy to train a Border collie. You not only need a lot of stamina but also a huge open field for him to run and exercise around. This may be one of the biggest reasons for not adopting a Collie if you live in an apartment. Border collie dog owner needs to be more active than the dog to meet up to his expectations. They are not only energetic but also very sensitive. A little scolding and they might just become super sad.

A package in itself, Border collie will keep your house chirpy and warm with its affection and energy for a healthy lifespan of 12-15 years. Be ready for a roller coaster ride!

Modern-day Border collie can trace back its legacy in one dog named Old Hemp (hell of a name for a dog, though). Widely considered to be the forefather of the entire breed, Old Hemp had a soft herding technique and is known to father 200 pups.

Border collie care

Provide them with exercise and mental stimulation. Border collie is not just an active dog but also a brainiac. If you fail to direct his energy and intelligence into something productive, he might develop destructive tendencies. Born workaholics, he needs exercise on a professional level, daily which should not be limited to walk.

Blending regular walking with one canine sport daily can keep him healthy and busy.

Border collie needs space. Being used to running in vast terrains for more than 50 miles a day, they need a similar space to wander even when domesticated. This means that they are not suited for apartment-style living. They need a large open field to run about and train for professional dog sport. Small places and congested flats can cause them discomfort and make them cranky.

Early socialization is a must. Border Collie is an introvert. And you know how introverts are? They just do not want to be friendly with anybody. So, if you want your Border Collie to get along well with other doggies in your neighborhood, he needs early socialization.

It doesn't just end here. They were born herders and tend to nip chasing animals or children at the heel. You need to make your Collie understand that it is not cool to be rough with children and other friendly pets. Precisely for this reason, it is more than necessary to expose them to children, cats, and other dogs since puppyhood.

Border Collie is highly trainable. With proper obedience training, you can control every movement of your dog. They will not only listen to your commands but also act the way you want them to act. This way you can also make them friendly with children and other pets.

Additionally, they are very sensitive dogs. You do not want to hurt their feelings. Praise and positive reinforcement techniques like giving them their favorite treat when they obey your command can work wonders.

Border Collie barks a lot. A little movement and they will inform you about it immediately. They may bark for every emotion they feel, be it fear, caution, or even if they need attention. You need to start controlling his barking habits since puppyhood so that it doesn't become a nuisance for your neighbors.

Border Collie is an attention-seeker. They need a lot of attention from their favorite person. Make sure you spend a lot of time cuddling and playing with him otherwise chances are that your puppy may suffer from separation anxiety and depression. If you have a tight working schedule and cannot make out time for your Collie, then you may not want to adopt him in the first place.

Border collie personality

When it comes to Border collie characteristics, there is a lot of fields to cover Adopting a Border Collie is like adopting a truckload of madness. Though they are arguably the world's smartest dogs, Border Collie temperament is not everyone's to handle. They are a very active and energetic dog. They have a habit of working all day in harsh weather conditions. This strong working drive can be exhausting for you sometimes.

Border Collies tend to get bored very easily. You cannot make them do same things twice which means you need to be creative enough to come up with a new job for them every day.

They like to keep themselves busy and if he is bored he might resort to digging, barking, or chasing. He needs to serve a purpose and he might go to any extend for that.

Bred as a herder, he may possess certain herding instincts like nipping small pets and children or chasing cars. A proper training since puppyhood and early socialization can control these habits. If you are his favorite person, he is more likely to obey you and learn commands at a faster speed to impress you.

Border collie dog is a very sensitive dog and will respond to even the slightest of the whistle of his favorite person. Be ready to get a reaction to every action of yours. They are very cautious of strangers. Alert with a ready bark, they make a wonderful watchdog.

Border collies can move swiftly in a catlike, crouched position because they have space between the tops of the shoulder blades, which lets them slither by while staying low to the ground. This technique lets them herd animals with extreme precision.

They are very shy and introverted dogs. Early socialization can help them overcome their reserved nature and may also control their nipping instincts. Proven to listen to command 95% of the time, Border collie intelligence has always been the talk of the town. Positive reinforcement training methods can help them in ways you never imagined. Smart and agile dogs, if trained properly and with patience, Border collie can stand out in every dog sport.

Additionally, they require a lot of attention from their family. Due to lack of enough affection, cuddles, and love, he might suffer from separation anxiety or depression. This means you are not only supposed to be his trainer-in-command but also his squishy soft-toy to cuddle with.

We have a step-by-step grooming procedure for these smarty pants.
Border Collie Coat Grooming

Step 1: Detangling Spray

Because Border Collies mostly like working out in rugged terrain, their coat may trap dirt and tangle their fur. Detangling spray can be used to minimize hair breakage in comparison to brushing dry fur. It softens the tangles and makes it easier to brush off his coat.

Step 2: Border collie Undercoat Grooming

Select a de-shedding tool of your choice (slicker brush or an undercoat rake) to remove dirt and fur exfoliation from his undercoat. Give several combs until you see zero sheds on the brush. Gentle brushing but firm pressure, that's exactly how you do it. This movement not only helps in circulation beneath the skin but also helps rejuvenate nourishing oils throughout the undercoat.

Step 3: Border collie Topcoat Grooming

Use a pin and bristle brush to groom his topcoat. Start with the pin side to remove all the shed and debris. Finally moving on to the bristle brush to give the

Step 4: Border collie Ear Cleaning

Look out for ear wax and give their ear a cleaning every time you plan to groom their coat. Unclean ears and excess ear wax can lead to injuries or infections. Consult your vet for the best ear products.

Step 5: Nail Trimming

Regular nail trimming is important. It helps your dog maintain a grasp of the ground and prevent him from slipping and getting injured. While you are at it, give a little trim to the hair around his nails. They tend to grow fast and long which may cause them discomfort.

Border collie grooming needs are minimalistic. A quick brushing twice a week and an occasional bath do it for him. They shed heavily twice a year fall and spring. You need to take extra care of his grooming during this time. You may want to shift from brushing twice a week to four times a week.

They have healthy teeth but to maintain that bright smile, you need to brush his teeth thrice or four times a week to avoid foul odor or tooth infection.

Border collie Feeding

Puppy Age (3-5 Months)

You must feed your Border Collie puppy at least three meals a day of ½ a cup of high-quality dry food.

Border Collie puppies need a minimum of 22% of protein and 8% of fat in their puppy food. They are an active breed and they require the right amount of nutrition. You may be feeding him according to his age but he may remain thin and hungry. Don't stop him from eating as long as he is burning all those intakes.

Adult Age (1-5 Years)

For an adult dog, the food intake steadily shifts to two meals a day of 1.5-2.5 cups of high-quality dog food per serving.

An active Border Collie engaged in sports will require 900-1000 calories a day. However, full-time herders will require 1400 calories per day.

Senior (5-8 Years)

Senior Border Collies become less active with a slower metabolism. You can either continue feeding in the same pattern or plan a senior dog diet. If your dog starts putting on weight, try feeding him a little less than regular. You can also steadily shift into a complete homemade dog food diet for senior dogs. It is healthy, cheap and you would know what you are feeding you, grown-up boy.

When compared to a 150 lb Great Dane who eats 1,500 calories a day, at less than a third the size, Border Collies really do burn a lot of energy.

Border collie health

Active dogs are mostly healthy dogs. But that does not mean they are not prone to certain health conditions.

1. Hip Dysplasia

Although mostly seen in larger breeds, it may be evident in other dogs too. It is a condition in which the thighbone doesn't fit into the hip socket causing constant friction between both. It leads to gradual degradation and eventual failure of the joint.

Symptoms may include decreased range of motion, reluctance in rising, "bunny-hoping" or loss of thigh muscle mass.

You may ask your breeder to provide you with a certificate of the parent's hip dysplasia tests. Feed your dog with enough calcium and fiber during his growing years to avoid bone-problems. Try not breeding dogs with hip dysplasia

2. Progressive Retinal Atrophy (PRA)

This is an eye disease that leads to degeneration of the retina, causing vision loss or complete blindness. The symptoms may not appear at early ages but it may include night blindness, bumping into things in dim light, or unwillingness to go into dark rooms. It is hereditary. Adopt your puppy from a responsible dog breeder that keeps a check on the breeding lot for such health conditions.

3. Epilepsy

While epilepsy is common in a lot of dog breeds, it is not always inherited. It is a neurological condition that may cause mild or severe convulsions.

Symptoms may include running frantically, rigid limbs, staggered, hiding, or losing consciousness.

Seizures are frightening, but the long-term prognosis of dogs with idiopathic epilepsy is generally very good. It is important to take your dog to a vet when you see such

4. Collie Eye Anomaly

It is an inherited, developmental disease mostly found in herding dogs like Collies, Australian Shepherds, and Border Collies. There is a mutation on the gene that determines the development of the eye which causes the blood vessels that support the retina to underdeveloped. It may also lead to partial or complete blindness.

Symptoms may include abnormally small eyeballs, sunken eyeballs, or bumping into things.

This usually occurs while your Border Collie puppy turns two. Sadly, there is no treatment for this condition.

5. Osteochondritis Dissecans (OCD)

An abnormal development of cartilage on the end of a bone in the joint is an inflammatory condition. There are chances of the diseased cartilage to separate from the base bone. It commonly affects the shoulders, elbow, hip, or knee joints.

Symptoms may include limping or laming in the affected leg, swollen joint, or warm to touch.

You need to consult the vet if you see such symptoms. It most severe cases it requires surgery.

It is not necessary that every Border collie has to go through these conditions. If taken care of like your toddler and adopted the puppy from a responsible breeder, such problems may hardly arise.

Get your puppy vaccinated with canine parvovirus and canine distemper in the initial 6-8 weeks followed by boosters after every 3 years.

Deworming is necessary. Ask your vet about a worming prevention plan between 2-12 weeks of your puppy.

Chapter two

Border collie mixes

Border Collies are a dog breed type well known for being very hardworking and are considered to be the world's most intelligent dog breeds in the Canine rankings of dog breed intelligence. As a working dog, they can be a handful to manage if they are not kept busy or properly exercised.

This is why Border Collie mixed breeds are gaining popularity around the world, and if you are wondering which Border Collie crossbreeds are best, this list breaks down 25 best Border Collies mixed with other pure breeds to produce an amiable mixed breed.

History, Information about Border collie Mixed Breeds.

Historically, the Border collie was bred as a working dog, and any of it's mixed crossbreeds are likely to inherit the workaholic trait which makes them not suitable for people who are less active or if you are classed as an older person.

Border Collies are energetic and constantly in need of regular exercises and games to keep them sharp and active.

Border collie Appearance

Border Collie 18 To 22 Inches Weight ranges between 30 and 55 Pounds

Collie 24-26 inches for male dogs, 22-24 inches for female Collies 60-75 Pounds

Border Collie Mixed Breed 1 foot, 6 inches to 1 foot 30 to 45 Pounds

Dog Breed Appearance Border collie is a medium-size dog

Border Collie dog breeds are majestic, adorable and irresistibly a charismatic combo to have as a crossbreed.

The Border Collie's height averages anywhere between 18 to 22 inches and with that height, they can weigh between 30 and 55 pounds.

Height and weight is the main difference between collies and Border Collies besides everything else! Collies are classified as large dog breeds while Border collies are medium dog breed considered to be smaller in their stature at their height and weight.

Many homes and families like the Border collie mixed breed as their first pet.

While there are numerous varying reasons, mixed Border collies tend to have a balanced, calmer and amiable temperament compared to their workaholic parents.

But that's not all! Some of the most common reasons why families get attracted to Border Collie and their mixed breeds is due to:

The Border Collie and their mixed crossbreed dogs are obedient to their owners when they have been trained right. This makes them easy to train and they understand command very quickly without having to repeat yourself too much.

They are built for work and they enjoy working for fun.

The Border Collie mixed dogs are loyal to their owners and tend to develop a tight bond with the whole family

Some people prefer crossing a border collie with another breed. Crossing this dog can produce a unique dog that can have yet more traits from the other parent.

In another way, since the Border collie is a very active dog, crossing it with another breed may produce a mixed breed that is more calmer which makes it suitable for people that are not very outgoing as well as old people.

There are many Collie mixed breeds and the type depends on the parents. Here are the Top Collie breeds that you can welcome into your home today.

1. Border Jack

The Border Jack is this unique dog breed produces from the Border collie mix and the Jack Russel Terrier breed. They are known to be very cute and have a very active athletic character.

Many families love Border Jacks as they are boistrous and agile as their parents.

They have almond like eyes which are very irresistible but these breeds can sometimes be different from one to the other based on appearance as some mixes have standing ears while others have floppy ears.

While this dog is less active, it will need a few exercises to keep fit.

2. Border Point

This dog has good tracking skills, which, along with their high speed, makes it ideal for hunting as well as herding.

This breed was produced from the Border collie and the Pointer which is common in the southeastern part of America.

The Border point breed has a very dominant collie breed so much that I would not recommend it as the best dog breed for the first time owners. This is shown through its athleticism and active nature so it is not suitable for people looking for a calm dog.

3. Bordernese

The bordernese have a thick and fluffy coat much like the Golden Chow Retriever Mix and can adapt in very cold climates. Its parents are the Bernese mountain dog and the Border collie.

These dogs are very playful and friendly. They are also great with adults as well as kids. They are loyal and sometimes display a protective character.

If you are looking for a dog that will be you companion and keep up to your activities as well as show a calm state, this is your dog.

4. Ski-Border

This breed originated from the American Eskimo dog and the Border collie mix. These dogs are very popular in the US and the western part of Europe.

They are very friendly to anyone and get along well with other pets as well. Though this breed is calmer, it is sometimes very playful as well.

5. Border Sheepdog

With its parents being the collie and the Shetland sheepdog, breed is a combination of both sheep herding dogs. They have a silky coat which closely resembles that of a sheep. These dogs are also well known to be fast runners which are excellent if you are a jogger.

The border sheepdog is very smart, intelligent and very easy to train. It makes a great companion.

6. Border Collie Cocker

This breed resulted from the combination of the collie and the Cocker Spaniel and they are a very unusual breed.

Their coats can vary from one to the other but they are usually medium sized dogs with the body of a collie and the head of a Cocker.

These dogs are also very strong, energetic and can run for a long time. They tend to bark very loudly and can make excellent watchdogs.

7. Border Newfie

This is a unique cute-looking breed which gets its name from its parent breeds which are the collie and the Newfoundland breeds.

Its calmness is a result of the Newfoundland genes and this makes them very friendly dogs. On the other side they tend to get playful when you take them out and they only need little exercises.

8. Bodacion

Known for its iconic Dalmatian spots, this breed was produced from the Dalmatian and the collie breeds. They are very rare so you will be lucky to own one of these unique breeds.

These are cute dogs who like challenges. In addition to that, they are friendly and affectionate which will make them an excellent family pet.

9. Shollie

This breed gets its name from the "German shepherd" and the "Border collie mix" which are its parents. These breeds are not very popular as other breeds hence demand for them is very low.

Regardless of that, they are cute dogs that are also very friendly.

The shollie is very smart and will require a lot of exercises to keep it fit. Other than that, they make excellent watchdogs.

10. Boxolie

This breed originated from the Boxer and the Border collie and are known for their cheerful character to their owners. Unlike other dogs, this breed will need less exercises but is a very fun dog to be around.

Their boxer genes make the Boxolie a very suspicious dog. This is a good trait for a watchdog.

They are also affectionate with their owners and good with kids. With their pack mentality, these dogs will protect you no matter what.

11. Golden Border Retriever

This balance between the Golden retriever and the collie make this dog popular in many households.

Since the golden retriever is one of the most loved dogs in America and well known for their service work, cross-breeding it with the intelligent collie is an idea that a lot of people love.

The collie genes make this dog calm and easy going. However it needs regular exercises to keep it from being too lazy.

Besides that, they are loyal dogs and have a happy temperament.

12. English Borsetter collie

This is a rare breed that originated from the English setter and the Border collie breeds.

These dogs are very athletic and can't seem to tire. Though being very energetic, their energy levels are less than that of a pure Collie breed.

The English Borsetter is a dog that needs a lot of exercises to keep their bodies fit.

Despite this, they seem to be affectionate to everyone in the family and make excellent pets.

13. Border Collie Benard

While being very friendly dogs, these breeds can sometimes be protective and will do all they can do keep their family from being hurt.

They are open to a lot of activities because they have so many great qualities from their parents.

They swim, hunt and even herd.

These dogs are very intelligent, fast and easy to train.

14. Border Schnollie

This is a breed that was produced from the Border collie and the Standard Schnauzer breed.

Since the Schnauzer comes in miniature and giant sizes as well, they can also be crossbred to produce Miniature Border Collie and Giant Border Collie.

The Border Schnollie dogs are popular in the United States and Surrounding regions. Their vast sizes come with different coat colors as well.

If you are looking for a dog that will do anything for you, get yourself a Border Schnollie. All they need is care and they will be your best friend.

15. Border Heeler

It is a combination of the Border Collie and the Blue Heller dogs which are the best active dogs as they are both good at herding.

Both of these dogs are also smart as they rank in the top 10 of the smartest dogs.

The Border Heller is an active dog that easily gets bored when it is not given attention.

It also needs a lot of exercise which has to be both physically and mentally. This makes them hard dogs to maintain.

Other than that, they are loyal to their owners and very affectionate.

16. Borgi

The short name is derived from its parents which are the Border Collie and the Welsh Corgi.

These dogs have short legs which is a result of the dominant Corgi genes.

The Borgi are very good at herding. They got this trait from both parents as they are great herders too.

This dog, like most Border collie mixes, requires a lot of exercises to keep it from being lazy because lazy dogs become obese in the long run. Despite this, they are overall intelligent dogs that are easy to train.

17. Border Collie Bull Staffy

This breed is a mixture of the Collie and the Staffordshire bull terrier which make very good guard dogs when they are properly trained.

They are known for being too loyal and courageous that they will sacrifice themselves for the benefit of their owners.

They are one of the bravest dogs and they inherit this trait from the Staffordshire bull terrier.

If you want a dog that will stick to you no matter what, this is the breed for you.

18. Border Pyrenees

Its parents are the Border collie and the Great Pyrenees breed. These breeds are rare so you are lucky to find such a type of mixed breed.

They have a large coat which helps keep them warm in the cold seasons as well as keeping them from the sun's heat in the hot climate.

They are what many people call "nanny dogs" because they are so good with children and need very minimal supervision.

19. Border Beagle

This is a mixed breed which was produced from the Border collie and the beagle.

The Border beagle has a long coat and goofy ears which come from the beagle gene.

Since the beagle is one of the most loved dogs in America and the United Kingdom, Border beagle is has increasingly become popular as well.

The long coat requires regular grooming. Despite that, it does not shed very much which makes this dog ideal for allergic people.

This breed has a happy personality and will be an excellent pet for you.

20. Border Collie Pit

This breed is a mixture of the Border collie and the pit bull terrier. These dogs are becoming very popular in homes because they are friendly and get along well with people as well as other pets.

They are very suspicious and alert dogs which makes them good watchdogs. They are also good at herding.

Despite their intimidating look, they are very loving dogs and will be by your side for a long time.

21. Border Collie Britt

This is a very energetic dog that loves to play all day. It is a mixed breed produced from the Border collie and the Brittany breeds.

However it is so rare and only a few people know that these dogs even exist.

They are independent and curious dogs so they tend to wonder out own their own.

On the other hand they need to have regular exercises to keep them active so if you like runs, take them with you.

The Border collie breed is very loyal and will make a faithful companion.

Also, the fact that it is rare means that it is unique so go out there and get yourself a Border collie Britt.

22. Border Springer

This increasingly popular dog is mixture of the Border collie and the English springer spaniel breeds. Its features are well noticeable as it has the body of a Springer spaniel and the coat is that of a Collie.

It also has markings that differ from dog to dog.

This breed is known to be versatile as it can be used for hunting, it can swim and also be a good companion. It is also very energetic and intelligent.

23. Border Aussie

This dog is highly energetic and runs at a high speed which makes it an excellent herding dog.

It was produced after cross-breeding the Border collie and the Australian shepherd which are known to have similar characteristics.

Both breeds are good at herding but the only difference is that the collie is good at herding sheep while the Australian shepherd is a cattle herder.

The Border Aussie has a very happy personality and will get along with just about everyone.

24. Great Collie

This mixed breed came from the Border collie breed and the Great Dane breed.

The Great Dane dog is called great because it is tall and has long legs. This gene is passed on to the mixed breed as well as they are also tall.

They are known for their high levels of energy and tend to jump on their owners.

This behavior can be controlled by training them to be obedient. Overall it is a playful, loving and affectionate dog that will go anywhere with you.

25. Afghan Collie

The Afghan Collie is one of the breeds that are most rare. Because of this, not many people know about them and documentaries only tell us little information on their existence but they deserve to be on this list.

They were originally bred in Afghanistan as its parents are the Border collie and the Afghan hound.

The Afghan Collie is one of the most versatile dogs as it can do just about anything.

They can hunt, play in competitions and be excellent guard dogs as well.

When it comes to Border collie mixes, choices are numerous and the top 25 breeds listed here, are a few of many you can have as your companions and family pets.

Farm Collie Definition

The term farm collie is frequently applied to any dog of the collie family that is either old fashioned in looks or that does farm work.

The original collie dog was the Highland Scotch Collie that helped with sheep herding in the Scottish Highlands from time immemorial until the Border collie took over in the early twentieth century. This was the original farm collie, born and bred for farm work and was definitely old-fashioned in looks beings that these were the olden days.

This is, in my perspective, the true farm collie, the Scotch Collie, registered today as the Old-Time Scotch Collie, the remnant of the old original Scottish collie dogs. Although the name "farm collie" is loosely used for a wide range of collie type dogs.

Farm Collie Breeds

From those original Scottish Highland Collies the rest of the collie family was bred, rough and Smooth Collies to meet the weird and arbitrary standards of the kennel clubs and the Border Collie for its peculiar crouching manner of moving sheep. The English Shepherd breed came about by crossing heavily with the shepherd dogs of England, the Australian Shepherd by crossing with Spanish shepherd dog. Other, more obscure collie types had similar histories, the collie spread out around the world and was bred to meet different needs and standards.

Today a farm collie could be any one of the following breeds or some combination of these breeds. In order to be farm collies however the dog must exhibit some of the old fashioned looks of the old Scotch Collies as well as their intelligence and working abilities (whether or not they actually live or work on a farm).

Old-Time Scotch Collie

Of these types the Old-Time Scotch Collie is the closest to the original collies of the Scottish Highlands and their breed association works to keep them that way without changing them to meet arbitrary standards. You can visit the Old-Time Scotch Collie Association website at this link to read about their activities and breeding program.

Pros

What are the advantages of farm collies? Here is a quick rundown of the reasons why in my opinion the farm collie is the perfect dog.

They are wicked smart

They are very laid back and not hyper

They are super human oriented

Intelligence – All collie breeds are known for their brains. The farm collie's smarts make it possible for them to pick up new commands quickly, puzzle out problems and anticipate your desires easily.

Calm – The farm collie is a work dog but unlike the Border Collie and some other dogs in this family, the farm collie is not high strung and does not need to be constantly occupied. They are content to lay about when there is no work to do but are also ready for activity at a minutes notice if there is a need.

People oriented – A farm collie wants to be with his or her people. The more time you spend with your farm collie the better results you will have. On the other hand, the more time you spend apart for your dog the more problems you will have. They always do best in homes where someone is at home most of the day, families that home school or work from home are especially successful with farm collies. Their human oriented personality make them especially obedient dogs as they want to please their people.

Cons

There are not many negatives to farm collies but here are a couple of the more common complaints.

They shed hair

They do not like being alone for long periods

They desire, even demand attention at times

All collie dogs have a hair problem, they shed and sometimes it feels like it is an unending supply of hair. I know some farm collie owners who have spun the collie hair into yarn and knitted sweaters out of it. It is a problem you must learn to live with if you have a collie of any kind.

A naughty collie is most likely one who has been left at home alone for long periods. They strongly desire to be with their humans, left alone they can start to chew things or cleverly escape kennels and in general make trouble. The best behavior will be obtained by spending a great deal of time with your farm collie.

A farm collie's human oriented behavior can be a good thing when you are calling them off of chasing a cat and they respond on the first call. However the other side of that coin is that they want lots of attention, if you do not have time to give a farm collie then perhaps a different breed would be best for you.

Farm Collie Puppies

Because a farm collie puppy can be any of several breeds you should be especially diligent when selecting a puppy. Ask the breeder all about the parents and their temperaments, even go meet those dogs in person if possible. Make sure that the parents meet your requirements for then type of dog you are looking for.

Farm collie puppies

Considerations

Bringing a new dog home is a big decision that requires a great deal of thought. Make sure you are fairly confident that yours will be a forever home before you make arrangements.

A farm collie may be unhappy if left home alone for long periods of time. You will find that they thrive best in homes with a stay at home parent, with homeschooled kids or with people who work from home. Still there are farm collies living in all kinds of situations, on farms, in cities and suburbs, farm collies that contentedly stay home alone all day and those that don't. The secret is understanding the landrace character of the farm collie (see this link which explains landrace) and finding a dog who has the characteristics to thrive in your situation. As I advised in the puppy section above, talk to the breeder.

Remember that the farm collie is still a rare breed, so it would be good if you would at least consider breeding one litter from your farm collie. Only by conscientious breeding will their numbers increase. If you do decide to breed you will find that the Old-Time Scotch Collie Association can help you to find good permanent homes for the puppies.

Border collie Colors

AKC Parent Clubs "own" the policy on whether or not their breed may, or is required to, be divided by color in conformation classes. In 2006, BCSA sent the following letter to AKC to update the policy on the Border Collie.

BCSA has gotten feedback from exhibitors that the color class division definitions for Border Collies were unclear and confusing. The current class divisions are "Black & White" or "AOAC." Exhibitors weren't always sure in which class to enter tri-colored dogs. Additionally, the word "allowed" in AOAC implied that there are some colors which are not allowed, yet in the Border Collie, any color is acceptable. So, BCSA convened a committee to review the subject and propose a course of action.

This committee requested membership input, analyzed how other breeds word color division definitions and came up with a proposed change to the class definitions. It was decided to continue to allow color divisions to hopefully raise awareness that our breed comes in many colors besides the traditional black and white "tuxedo" markings and that there are no disallowed or less-preferred colors. However, we understand that at many all-breed shows, the Border Collie entry is too small to justify class division, so will continue to leave it at the show-giving club's discretion on whether or not to divide.

We would just like to change the color definitions for those times when show-giving clubs do choose to divide on color. When a division is offered, only the Open classes shall be divided. The color classes shall be Black (including Black & White and Tri-Color). All Other Colors or AOC (note: remove the word "allowed" in the acronym).

A GUIDE TO THE GENETICS OF COLOR

The purpose of this guide is to provide some very basic information regarding the influence of genetics on coat color. It is important to emphasize that this subject is complex and confusing at best. Research is ongoing and what may be the prevailing theory today, may well be disproved in the future.

The genetics of color is a fascinating subject, which has been oversimplified here, in the hopes that the material is understandable and useful. If you would like to see examples of the colors mentioned, please visit our Breed Color pages above.

There are individuals who have put a great deal of time and energy into the study of "color" genetics and the information found on their websites is very informative and much more detailed than you will find in this guide. Understanding concepts of inheritance must first start with learning to speak the "language" of genetics.

IT STARTS WITH DNA

In sexual reproduction, genetic material from the sire and dam are passed on to their offspring in the form of DNA. The makeup of DNA consists of two strands of genetic material that connect to each other forming what is known as "base pairs". How these base pairs align with each other, become the genetic blueprint for a particular trait. These aligned base pairs of DNA (one from each parent) are called GENES. Genes are located within chromosomes. A GENE LOCUS is where a gene is located on a chromosome. One published analogy likened a chromosome to a music CD; the genes found on the chromosome, occupy a specific location or "locus" much like music is found on a specific track. This is an important concept to keep in mind when we talk about the different GENE SERIES OR LOCI later in this guide.

PHENOTYPE: Phenotypes are the physical characteristics, created by the combination of genes that can be "observed" about an individual (such as hair or eye color).

GENOTYPE: The genetic makeup of an individual created by the combination of genes. Not all of

ALLELE: Different versions of a gene for the same trait, such as color, which gives rise to different phenotypes, are known as alleles. The individual will have two alleles for each trait as one is inherited from each parent. Alleles may be dominant or recessive.

DOMINANT AND RECESSIVE: An allele is dominant if it "show's itself" and hides the presence of another allele. For example, if a dog has a copy of a black gene and copy of a brown** gene, the dog will be black because black is dominant to brown (recessive). You cannot tell by looking at the dog if they have a copy of the brown gene (genotype). An allele is recessive if its effect is not seen when a more dominant allele is present, as in the brown example above. For the dog to be brown, he must have two copies of the brown gene.

** NOTE: in the United States, the traditional nomenclature for a Border collie that is brown in color is to call them RED and they are registered as such. However, due to the fact that they are considered "brown" genetically (genetic code "bb"), that is the term that will be used in this guide.

HETEROZYGOUS: When the two genes making up an allele are different, such as "Bb" (Black as dominant and brown as recessive), it is referred to as being heterozygous for that gene.

HOMOZYGOUS: When the two genes making up the allele are identical, such as "bb" (both genes recessive for brown), it is referred to as being homozygous for that gene.

Therefore, when a dog is heterozygous for a specific gene, statistically it will pass the dominant copy to half its offspring and the recessive copy to the other half. When it is homozygous for a particular gene, it will pass this copy to its entire offspring.

COLORS AND PATTERNS

The substance that gives a dog's hair its color is called MELANIN. There are two types of melanin in the dog:

EUMELANIN: The dark pigments of Black and Brown

PHAEOMELANIN: A yellow or red color

Note: Both of these pigments can be acted upon by other genes, thereby altering these "base" colors (discussed later).

Only the dominant version of the color gene results in eumelanin production. If the dog has two copies of the recessive version, he will have no eumelanin, and his hair will contain only the light pigment. His nose leather and eye rims will be red or brown.

There are also Pattern genes that affect the distribution of a particular color on the dog. Both the color and pattern of a dog is determined by several Loci or gene series. There is no "single" gene that dictates coat color, but rather a combination of genes that are either expressed or carried that determines the color and pattern of the offspring.

The following is a very basic discussion that addresses some, but not all, of the Loci and the influence they exert in the total "equation" that makes up colors and patterns. Included in some cases, will be the genetic "coding" used to represent part or all of a dog's color genotype but it is NOT an all-inclusive list of the genetic possibilities.

A (Agouti): This locus is responsible for how the pigment is distributed along the dog's hair shaft and body regions, by inhibiting eumelanin (dark pigment) production. This locus is involved with Sable dogs (both shaded and clear), Saddleback Sable, and "Tan points".

Dominant Black (K)

This gene turns the "Agouti" genes on and off and codes are:

Black (Agouti genes "off"; not expressed) and

Brindle (Agouti genes "on; expressed) code: br^k

As well as combinations of the above as "expressed" or "carried"

Example: K^br is a black dog carrying brindle. Kk^Ayat is a black dog carrying sable and tricolor

Brindle is a pattern of alternating stripes of eumelanin and phaeomelanin pigmentation (yellow/black, or red/black)

B Locus (Brown): This gene determines or selects for a black or brown dog. When this gene is in its dominant form (BB or Bb) the dog is black. When this gene is in its homozygous recessive form (bb) it has a lightening effect on the eumelanin only and the dog is brown.

BB is homozygous Black (not carrying brown)

Bb is heterozygous Black (carrying brown)

Bb is homozygous Brown.

D Locus: This dilution gene acts on both eumelanin and phaeomelanin pigments. It "dilutes" the base color of the dog. If the dog is "D" or dominant, it is fully pigmented. If the dog is "dd", this recessive gene dilutes the pigment, thereby altering its color. In Border Collies, the d/d gene is associated with skin problems such as Color Dilution Alopecia or hair loss (on the ears is common) which can be seen in the Blue and Lilac dogs. If the Dilution gene acts on the brown and black coats, you can get the following: black diluted to blue and brown diluted to lilac (see photo to right).

Lilac is caused primarily by a "double recessive" condition of bb at the B gene locus and dd at the dilute gene locus. It is also possible to produce a

110

Lilac color out of pairings of black-to-black, black to brown, brown-to-brown, black to blue and blue to brown IF the genes are paired correctly AND they both carry the recessive forms of the B and the D gene ("b" and "d")

To demonstrate the genetic possibilities as mentioned above, let's make both the sire and the dam genotypes the same as BbDd. These black dogs carry both brown and the dilution gene.

In this case, Black is dominant (B). If it is acted on by the dilution gene (dd), it will produce a Blue dog. Brown is recessive (bb) and if it is acted on by the dilution gene (dd), it will produce a lilac dog. If the black or the brown dog has Dd, where D indicates the dog is fully pigmented, they retain their base color.

If we were to express the above diagram in statistical probability: 56% of the offspring would be black, 19% would be brown, 19% would be blue and 6% would be lilac. Keep in mind that the example above is only showing the B and D gene series effect on the genotype. Other gene series influence and are a part of the total "picture". If the Dilution gene acts on the light coat (phaeomelanin) it will dilute a red color to cream (for the description of the red color, see the E locus).

E Locus: This gene series either restricts or extends pigments in the hair follicle. If it is in its dominant form (E), it extends the darker pigment (Black or Brown dog). If it is in its recessive form (e/e), it allows only the extension of the phaeomelanin, and the dog's color becomes what is called a TRUE RED, Australian Red or in the United States, "Gold".

This gene is considered a "masking" gene as it will hide a dog's true color. However, it only affects the hair follicle so you can identify its color by the nose leather and eye rims. For example, a dog that is genetically Brown will have brown or reddish nose leather /eye rims but has a golden to red coat color. If it also has the dilution gene, the coat will be a creamy color. Its genetic code might look like "b/b, d/d, e/e".

S Locus: The S gene series demonstrates various patterns of white spotting. This includes the traditional white markings seen on black border collies, often called Tuxedo Markings or Irish spotting as well as the piebald spotting pattern and the extreme white spotting pattern.

The coding is as follows:

S^i tuxedo markings

S^p piebald spotting where there are random spots of color on a white background.

S^w a dog that is almost completely white.

Currently, Border Collies that have extreme amounts of white and or white that crosses the flank in lines or patches are referred to as being "white factored." Having increased white areas is not a problem per se, however, from a breeding perspective, there is research-linking deafness to the alleles for piebald spotting or extreme whiteness.

T Locus: The T series refers to "ticking" or flecks of color in white areas. Code for Ticked is T^T (and non-ticked is t/t)

M locus: The Merle gene is a pattern gene, not a color in of itself. It is also a dilution gene. It causes patchy areas of color dilution, resembling a marble-like pattern. This will result in a genetically black dog to show grey patched with black areas and they will have a black nose. If the dog is genetically blue, he will have grey patched with dark blue/grey areas and a grey nose (commonly called a Slate Blue). Both are referred to as BLUE

114

MERLES. A genetically brown dog will show patchy cinnamon/brown/red patches and they will have a liver colored nose (RED MERLE). A genetically SABLE dog would be called a SABLE MERLE, however, with the phaeomelanin dominating the color scheme, they are often difficult to recognize as adults.

Only a merle parent can produce a merle puppy...It is not a gene that is "carried", therefore, the coding would be M for Merle or "m" for non-merle.

Breeding a merle to merle is not recommended as the offspring can have a significant risk of health problems.

General characteristics of the Border collie

Border Collies love to serve people. They give a charge of positive emotions, are constantly active and cheerful. They will accompany the owner in sports, take an active part in his life. But at the same time, the Border collie is an agreeable, obedient, and friendly dog. He loves children, takes care of and herds them, anticipates the wishes of the owner, and is not annoying.

The nature and habits of the Border collie

The border is a hard worker. It is ideally suited for long hours of work in nature, for the long run, for the master's commands. The job of a shepherd requires that the dog is not picky about food and the ability to patiently endure any weather conditions. As a guard, she has an excellent instinct and can drive away a predator that has encroached on her herd.

He treats people with understanding, wariness, but without aggression and hysteria when meeting strangers. Loyal and attentive to the owner, ready to carry out any of his commands. It learns well but is able to make decisions on its own and even manipulate the owner. It is considered one of the most intelligent breeds. Recommended for agility competition, which goes through the obstacle course, guided by the orders and gestures of the owner.

Character

Border Collies can run all day long, enjoying the owner's command. Their intuition and fearlessness make them vigilant watchmen. They can be trusted to guard the house, but this collie will not become an evil chain dog. Borders get along well with other pets, even cats or rodents. Become a leader for them, will shepherd and protect.

By nature, the dog is friendly, affectionate, very loyal. She loves to lead the owner, accompany him everywhere, as she is very curious. But she will never be imposed, she is not inclined to the violent manifestation of emotions.

All outsiders are wary, but not aggressive. There is absolutely no cowardice, nervousness, or anger in the character. She loves children, will be their devoted friend, vigilant guard, and nanny. She will never offend even a small child, and the student will become a companion and companion in any outdoor games.

Features of education

This dog is quick and easy to train. Likes to execute commands, but is able to act independently, make decisions. High intelligence allows her to manipulate the owner, so it is important to gain authority. If the puppy is not raised, the activity of the mental abilities will make him uncontrollable. But even an adult dog can be taught the rules of behavior. Only for this is the owner's patience and love important.

Borders are easy to train, they enjoy learning, teams enjoy. They especially love to exercise on simulators, to run. But if the pet gets bored, he will stop obeying. Therefore, the puppy needs to be interested, it is better to train in the game. During training, physical activity or an aggressive tone should not be applied. The dog understands the words perfectly and he needs a calm, friendly attitude.

Difficulty can be caused by the strong herding instincts of these dogs. Already at the age of six months, they begin to graze everyone around, driving them into a heap, often for this they grab the legs with their teeth. This desire must be immediately stopped. The peculiarity of upbringing is also that the border requires the firmness and authority of the owner. Only then will he not strive to dominate and will be obedient.

Care

Border Collie dogs are unpretentious, easily adaptable to any conditions. They are picky about food, tolerate bad weather well. It is best to start them for a country house, only to settle them in a large aviary, and not on a chain. You can also keep a border collie in an apartment, but if you don't walk it, it will get bored.

At home, the pet should have its own place with bedding. It must be located away from drafts and radiators. It is desirable that from a place the border can behave behind the owner since this dog does not like loneliness. Be sure to buy the puppy toys, otherwise, he may start gnawing things out of boredom

It is necessary to walk with the dog at least 2-3 hours a day. Without sufficient physical activity, he will lose his working qualities. It is better to walk on the dog playground so that the pet overcomes obstacles. These dogs are very fond of running after sticks, a ball. In summer it is recommended to go to the river.

Nutrition

The diet of the dog should be chosen to take into account its hyperactivity. You can feed the border with dry food or natural food, the main thing is to choose the right portion size. The pet must receive the necessary vitamins, minerals, fatty acids.

The diet should contain;

Meat, offal, poultry, sea fish;

Cereals, as a source of carbohydrates, buckwheat or rice porridge is better;

Vegetable fiber — spinach, apples, zucchini, cabbage;

Vegetable oil;

Once a week — an egg, dairy products.

Many owners choose dry food, in which case it must contain at least 50% protein. It is necessary to give preference to topics designed for active dogs. They should contain Omega 3 fatty acids, fiber, vitamins, preferably chondroitin for joint support. The composition should not contain soy, corn, and wheat, as these dogs are prone to allergies.

Pros

The main characteristics are extremely positive, but there are several important advantages to note.

Mind and training. Enough has been said about the intelligence of the collie. From this it follows that they are easy to train, they quickly master commands.

Working ability. You can use the Border collie not only as friends but also as colleagues. This is true for service people. Also an interesting fact – you can hunt and take a dog with you.

The possibility of home content. There are breeds that do not work. These are often referred to as husky and shepherd dogs. This impossibility is connected rather with the fact that not everyone can adjust the microclimate at home to the atmosphere of a dog. Collie won't be a problem! They were bred to help humans, and therefore get along well with people.

Suitable pet character. Everyone wants just such a dog – funny, loving to run, play.

The average size. To be honest, keeping a large dog in the house is an incredibly difficult task. Keeping a big dog in an apartment is simply unrealistic. It is extremely difficult to arrange comfort and at the same time make sure that the pet does not destroy the entire home. It is advised to keep small or medium-sized dogs in

apartments. The Border collie fits this criterion —
the breed is among the average.

Cons

When describing the advantages of the Border
collie, one should pay attention to the
disadvantages. Inquiring about the presence of
negative traits of the desired pet is advised for all
owners.

The need for training. If the owner has no desire
instead of a friend to get a hyperactive clockwork
toy that absolutely does not listen to commands
and does not understand orders, then you will
have to train the pet.

A lot of time to leave. Training, daily routines to
maintain your appearance are time-consuming
events. In addition, a long walk.

Demanding wool. Collies are long-haired and smooth-haired. Both those and others require daily combing of the wool cover.

Excessive independence. Even an obedient and trained dog is difficult to instill the need to measure the territory that can be run. Therefore, there are frequent cases when representatives of this breed run away. In the best case, the escape will be short and the dog will return soon. At worst, the dog can be lost forever.

The Border collie is a lovely breed that definitely deserves attention. However, the owner of the animal must be prepared to face the possible consequences of his decision. The pluses of such dogs widely overlap the minuses, which indicates the reasonableness of the choice in their favor.

To start or not here is a philosophical question, which is answered by the person who wants to become a dog lover. The truth is that the four-legged is ready to become the best, loyal companion and friend who will not leave the person who sheltered him in any trouble and will support him in any joy.

10 Things You Need To Know Before Adopting a Border Collie

Adopting a dog can be incredibly confusing. After all, there are many breeds and personalities to choose from that picking one can feel next to impossible.

While adopting any dog from a shelter is undoubtedly a good deed, you can make the decision a lot easier on yourself if you have a specific breed in mind. Today we're going to go over Border Collies. You're about to learn what makes them an incredible breed, why they're the perfect fit for a family as well as some important information you need to know before signing the adoption paperwork.

1. Border Collies Are Full Of Energy

If you're looking for an athletic dog with incredible endurance and unbelievable energy, a Border Collie would likely be the perfect new addition for your home. Keep in mind, regular walks are a must with this breed. Keeping them pent up in a small area for long periods of time can lead to an overload of energy which can lead to negative behaviors. Make sure your new friend has plenty of space to run and burn off some of that fuel.

2. They're Highly Intelligent

Border Collies are incredibly smart. This is definitely a breed that you want to keep engaged and occupy with stimulating tasks. Training is a perfect way to achieve this. Border collie's are known to enjoy pleasing their humans and they're also known to have a strong desire to work. This combined with their amazing level of intelligence makes training simple and enjoyable.

3. You'll need To Keep Your Eye Out

Dogs are quite similar to humans when it comes to their genetics making them prone to certain health conditions. Generally speaking, this is a breed that often lives a long and healthy life with no health problems. However, there is the possibility that your new fur baby may be one of the unlucky few. While there's no way to tell if your Collie will be at risk or not, you can keep your eye out for certain signs and symptoms.

Important things to look out for would include poor mobility, bad eyesight, hearing loss and seizure activity.

4. Collies Are Easy To Groom

You may think when looking at a Border Collie that they require a great deal of grooming due to their medium length coat, but surprisingly, that's not the case at all. Occasional baths are recommended, typically one per month. You also might want to consider brushing their teeth twice per week, but it isn't required. One of the perks this breed has is their minimal shedding. Once a week brushing will keep your home clean and hair free.

5. A High Protein Diet Is a Must

As mentioned before, Border Collies are an extremely active breed. For this reason, they thrive best when supplied with a diet that is high in protein. This will give their muscles the nutrients they need to stay strong and healthy. Aside from protein, carbs are also important in a Collie's diet. The ideal diet consists of a high-carb, high-protein meal in the morning followed by a high-protein meal in the evening. Typical serving sizes range between 1 ½ – 2 cups of food split into two meals daily.

6. Socializing Has Its Benefits

Socializing your furry little friend has a ton of benefits. For example, it gives them playtime to burn off excess energy. Also, socializing is a great way to prevent your Collie from becoming shy and aggressive toward other animals. While this breed tends to be quite friendly and easy to get along with, they are known to show occasional aggression toward dogs of the same gender. Just make sure you supervise your buddy's play time.

7. Cats Are "Iffy"
Border Collie with cats in the same home.

While there is a great possibility that a Border Collie and a cat will get along just fine, interactions should always be monitored. Being a herding dog, your Collie may feel the need to try and corral your feline. Needless to say, this is not something your cat will enjoy.

8. Breeder Vs. Shelter

While a breeder may seem like the better option, that's actually not the case at all in most situations. First of all, there's likely a Border Collie in a shelter near you that would do anything for a chance at their own forever home. On top of that, purchasing a Collie from a breeder can easily cost $2,000 or more! On the other hand, adoption fees typically range between $50 and $100. So, when you adopt, you'll save a life as well as a lot of cash.

9. Border Collies Can Be Motivating

Believe it or not, bringing home a Collie may give you the motivation you need to break out of a rut. Their large supply of energy will require you to get up off of the couch and get moving. Soon enough this will become a habit. You'll be feeling great before you know it and your new friend will as well.

10. They're Kid Friendly

Border Collies are great with kids. They know how to play without being too rough. Plus, their loyalty drives them to protect children which is a huge advantage in the crazy world we live in today. However, small children should be taught how to properly play with their furry BFF. Tail pulling, sitting on their backs or other types of inappropriate behavior from children can lead Collies into becoming timid and in some cases even aggressive.

This is an excellent breed for an active family, especially one that has kids who love to play. Minimal grooming, a heart of gold, unmatched loyalty and the burning desire to please humans are just a few of the reasons why a Collie would make a great addition to nearly any family.

Chapter three

conclusion

So there you have it. You now have a great idea of which breeds work well with Border Collies and how you can go about figuring that out with your Collie yourself.

As always, getting a second dog is a big responsibility and shouldn't be any less important than getting your first. A second dog shouldn't just be to keep the first dog company and you and your family are responsible for loving, caring, and showing just as much time and attention to the second dog, as you did with your first.

Made in the USA
Middletown, DE
25 November 2022

16021650R00076